A Bug In

Ian Bland lives in Rossendale, Lancashire with his wife Kathryn and two loud and scary children called James and Madeleine. Over the last ten years he has visited hundreds of schools, libraries and festivals to perform his work and lead exciting poetry workshops.

When not writing poems you'll find Ian running around a tennis court getting heavily beaten by five-year olds, or cleaning up after his very messy kids.

For a poetry day at your school, Ian can be found on the web at **www.ianbland.com**

Philip Waddell has been pestering everyone for blank sheets of paper ever since he can remember. Luckily for his mum, a pencil and sketchbook would keep him quiet for hours. She wasn't quite so pleased when her nice, white kitchen walls also kept him quiet!

When not writing or drawing, Philip holds the world record for frisbeeing teabags (the round ones of course) across the kitchen and into mugs. He lives near Oxford with his kind and understanding wife.

A Bug In My Hair!

Poems by Ian Bland and Philip Waddell

Hands Up Books

British Library Cataloguing in Publication Data.
A catalogue record for this book is available from The
British Library.

ISBN 978-0-9555589-1-7

First Published 2009 by
Hands Up Books
1, New Cottages
Spout Hill
Brantingham
HU15 1QW
East Riding of Yorkshire
Email:handsup@handsup.karoo.co.uk

Printed in England by York Publishing Services Ltd

Contents

A Bug In My Hair!

A bug on the rug
A bug on my bed
A bug that has jumped
It's now on my head!

A bug on my head?
A bug in my hair?
Go away bug
You can't live up there!

Noisy Start

Alarm clock Brrrings
Shower Splishes
Sister Sings
Curtain Swishes.

Teacup Tinkles
Milk Slip-Slops
Paper Crinkles
Toaster Pops.

Teapot Rattles
Brother Slurps
Radio Prattles
Baby Burps.

Brother Moans
Workman Drills
Someone phones –
Mobile Trills.

BLAH BLAH

RATTLE

Dad, 'Kiss Kisses,'
Baby Cries
Mum, 'Shush Shushes,'
Mum, 'Goodbyes.'

Noisy aren't we
In the morn?
Off goes Daddy...
Toot Toots horn!

CRINKLE

SPORT DAILY NEWS

CRINKLE

3

The Mystery Game

I know how to play Conkers
And how to play Mouse Trap,
I know how to play Football
And love a game of Snap.

I'm champ at Chinese Checkers
And big at Buckaroo,
I'm good at Snakes And Ladders
And ace at Skittles too.

I play I Spy and Ludo
But one game's new to me -
It's one my Mum wants me to play...
Some game called... Quietly?

Play Quietly!

Obstacle Race

Over skittles

          Beneath the ropes

Slide down benches

             Time to sprint

    Avoid the hoops

            Catch the ball

   Lift the spoon up

            Egg on top

  Really steady

            Almost

there

        Classmates scream

                Easy

winner!

Why Can't I?

My sister goes to Guides
My brother goes to swim
My sister rides a horse
My brother goes to gym
My sister has a ring
My brother wears a tie!
Why can't I?

My daddy drives the car
My mummy cooks the chips
My daddy walks the dog
My mummy paints her lips
My daddy pours the drinks
My mummy cuts the pie!
Why can't I?

My Rocket Ship

T
Od
Ay I
Made
A rocket ship
That can fly
Me to the stars.
It's made from
Plastic bottles
Cardboard boxes
And jam jars.
Its engine is a
Broken
Clock,
That was left under the stairs.
The seats are made from socks and shirts
That no-one   ever wears.

Doing The Rounds

The second hand races
Around our clock faces -
Each minute one lap it will run.

The minute hand, slower,
Goes round once an hour
Like someone out jogging for fun.

The hour hand trails,
Like the plodder who tails -
Just two laps a day it will slog.

Slow as me round the green
When out strolling I've been -
Walking my little brown dog.

Strange Happenings!

Miss Hall come quick
I swear it's true
A monkey
In the infants loo!
And over in the library
A crocodile
Is drinking tea!
Some seals
Are swimming in the hall
They're playing with a basketball!
And in the corridor I swear
The most enormous
Grizzly bear!

Is this all happening in our school?
Of course it's not you
APRIL FOOL!

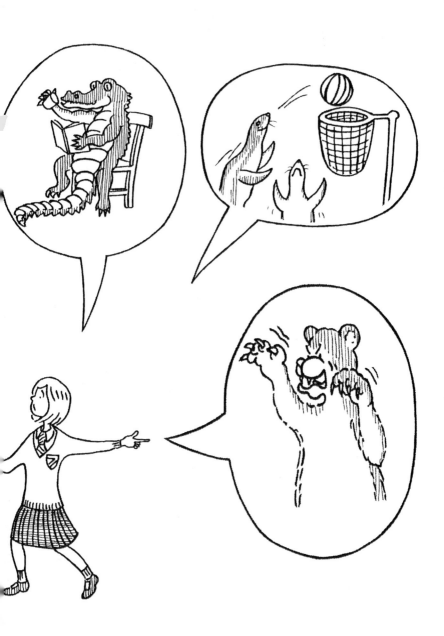

Can You Do It?

Clap clap with your hands

Sniff sniff with your nose

Stamp stamp with your feet

Tiptoe with your toes.

Blink blink with your eyes

Shake shake with your hips

Bend bend with your knees

Kiss kiss with your lips!

Raindrops

Raindrops raindrops
Drip drop drip
Falling falling
Plip plop plip.

Raindrops raindrops
Drop drip drop
Falling falling
Just won't stop!

Little Raindrop

Little raindrop, pitter pat,
Just been born, so small and cute.
Little raindrop, pitter SPLAT!
Shame you had no parachute!

Ten Pin Bowling

Take a run, roll the ball
Watch those skittles dance and fall!

Knock them down, Knock them down
Got to knock those skittles down!

Move your feet down the aisle
Smash those skittles down in style!

Knock them down, Knock them down
Got to knock those skittles down!

Lift that ball, fingers in
The swerve, the crash, the roar, the din!

Knock them down, Knock them down
Got to knock those skittles down!

Ten Bright Balloons

My first bright balloon
Bounced upon a bee.
The bee stang - BANG.

My second bright balloon
Floated to the sky,
Way up high. Bye!

My third bright balloon
I gave a crying child,
That child smiled.

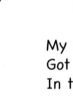

My fourth bright balloon
Got stuck up in a tree.
In that tree - *see!*

My fifth bright balloon
Sprang a little leak
Just like this - Hissss.

My sixth bright balloon
I filled with water
From a vat - SPLAT.

My seventh bright balloon
Just like magic
Disappeared! Weird.

My eighth bright balloon
I blew far too big,
Should have stopped - POPPED.

My ninth bright balloon
Someone said was theirs!
So... who cares? Tears.

My tenth bright balloon...
Didn't get a tenth -
Mum said NO! Ohhhh!

My Mum's Love

My Mum's love is :
Warmer than freshly popped toast,
Deeper than the leisure centre swimming pool,
Stronger than the chains
                on the playground swings,
Wider than the supermarket car park,
Sweeter than a strawberry Sundae
                with extra syrup,
Kinder than auntie Penny
                who always gives me a pound,
More fun than Children's TV,
Cosier than a snugly, bedtime hug.

I Think I Got Mixed Up!

Swimming in the garden
Digging in the pool
Taking sums to Gran's house
Having tea at school

Drinking with my knife and fork
Eating with my cup
You really must excuse me
I think I got mixed up!

Ivy Says

The parade is passing
But I can't see
With the forest of legs
Surrounding me.

So up his trunk,
From the bough of his knee,
I climb my dad
Who's as tall as a tree.

Don't Yawn Like Venus Flytrap!

Don't yawn like Venus Flytrap -
It isn't nice or wise.
If you yawn like Venus Flytrap
You're likely to catch flies!

See At The Zoo

Gape at ape
Spy aye-aye
Glare at bear
Pore over boar
Crane at crane
Peer at deer
Glance elephants
Gaze at gazelle
Peruse gnus
Stare at hare
Inspect insects
Peek-a-boo kangaroo
Sight kite
See kiwi
Regard leopard
Scrutinise magpies
Spot ocelot
Look at rook
Peep at sheep
Glimpse shrimps
Gawp *whaup
View zebu

* Whaup: a type of bird

Animal Alliteration

One purring pussy cat prowling by a wall

Two crazy kangaroos kicking round a ball

Three mischievous monkeys squirting lemonade

Four lazy lionesses lounging in the shade

Five diving dolphins dashing through the sea

Six sprightly squirrels scampering up a tree

Seven surly scorpions sitting on the sand

Eight enormous elephants exploring the land

Nine nibbling natterjacks nattering with a newt

Ten furry foxes fighting for some fruit!

I Like...

I like custard
I like jelly
I like eatin' it watchin' telly!

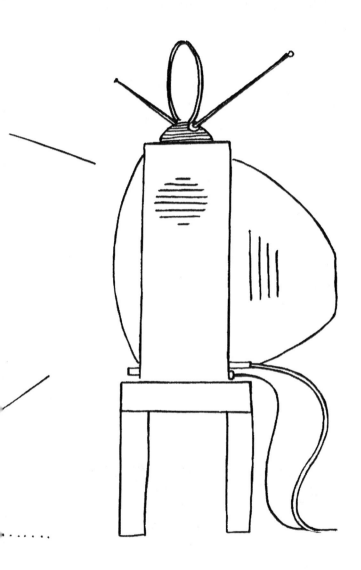

The Dental Drill
(To be recited whilst marching on the spot.)

Lovely stuff!
Minty taste!
Onto brush
Squeeze toothpaste.

Forward face
Teeth on guard!
Start to brush
(Not too hard!)

Brush those teeth
Left and right
Up and down
Nice and bright.

Water slurp
Sloosh about
Cheek to cheek
Spit it out.

Do this drill
Morn and night
Healthy teeth
Mighty bite!

Cared for teeth
Feel no drill
Flash that smile!
Fillings nil!

Ha Ha Ha Ho Ho Ho Hee Hee Hee Hee

At bedtime Oscar Octopus
Always gets the giggles,
Cos when his Mummy tucks him in
She does it with ten tickles!

37

What Am I?

A silvery disc a misty light
I sometimes will appear at night
Some say I might be made of cheese
I have craters mounts and seas
Just look for me up in the sky
What am I?

Grandparents' Gifts

Our Grandfather Sun
Has wished us 'Goodnight'
And gone home to bed –
He brings us daylight.

Now Grandmother Moon
Has paid us a call
With bags of sweet dreams
To treat one and all.

DREAMS

Bedtime Mysteries

Does Little Red Riding Hood
Rescue her gran?
Is the Pied Piper
A kindly young man?
Do Hansel and Gretel
Escape from the witch?
Do Jack's magic beans
Make the simple lad rich?
Is Goldilocks eaten up
By the three bears?
Are tortoises faster
At racing than hares?
Is the old woman
In Snow White a fake?
Don't ask me, I don't know,
I can't stay awake!

Little Miss Muffet

Little Miss Muffet
Sat on her tuffet
Eating a strawberry pavlova
Along came a spider and
Sat down beside her
And ate the bits she had left over!

Cats

They snuggle up with
Purr and paw
So mighty glad
To greet yer.

But if they were
Much bigger
I bet they'd want
To eat yer!

Monsters!

Big heads
Big feet
Big hands
Big seats
Monsters!

Sharp teeth
Sharp nails
Sharp ears
Sharp tails
Monsters!

With scales
With wings
With horns
With stings
Monsters!

44

And moles
And warts
And stinks
And snorts
Monsters!

Some mean
Some mad
Some kind
Some sad
Monsters!

Care Crow Sam

See that figure over there
Standing in the open air
Weather foul or weather fair?
That's Care Crow Sam - who will not scare.

When the farmer stood him there
It was to make the crows beware -
But round they flock, who shouldn't dare,
Unless, of course, the farmer's near.

Sam's arms say, there's a welcome here!
They say, I've lots of grain to share
So drop in if you've time to spare -
Your company brings me such cheer.

See that figure over there
Crowned with straw instead of hair?
That's Care Crow Sam who will not scare...
The answer to a raven's prayer.

Humpty Dumpty

Humpty Dumpty packed up his case
Humpty Dumpty flew off to space
The king's men called Humpty for all they were worth
But Humpty just wouldn't
Come back down to Earth!

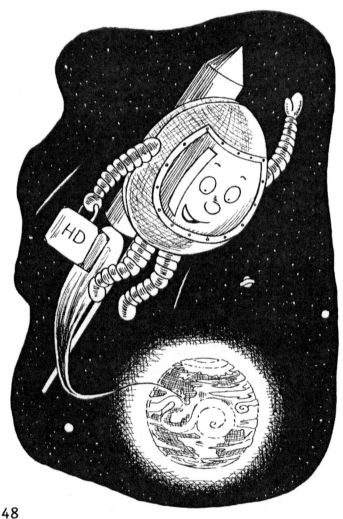

Ian's Poems

Phil's Poems

Acknowledgements

Ian's Poems:

My Rocket Ship, *Magnificent Machines*, Macmillan Children's Books, 2000.

Strange Happenings, *Funny Poems*, Scholastic Children's Books, 2003.

Little Miss Muffet, *Ha! Ha! 100 Poems To Make You Laugh*, Macmillan Children's Books, 2001.

Phil's Poems:

Ivy Says, *Here's A Little Poem*, Walker Books, 2007.

Bedtime Mysteries, *The Jumble Book*, Macmillan Children's Books, 2009.

Monsters!, *Read Me Out Loud!*, Macmillan Children's Books 2007.